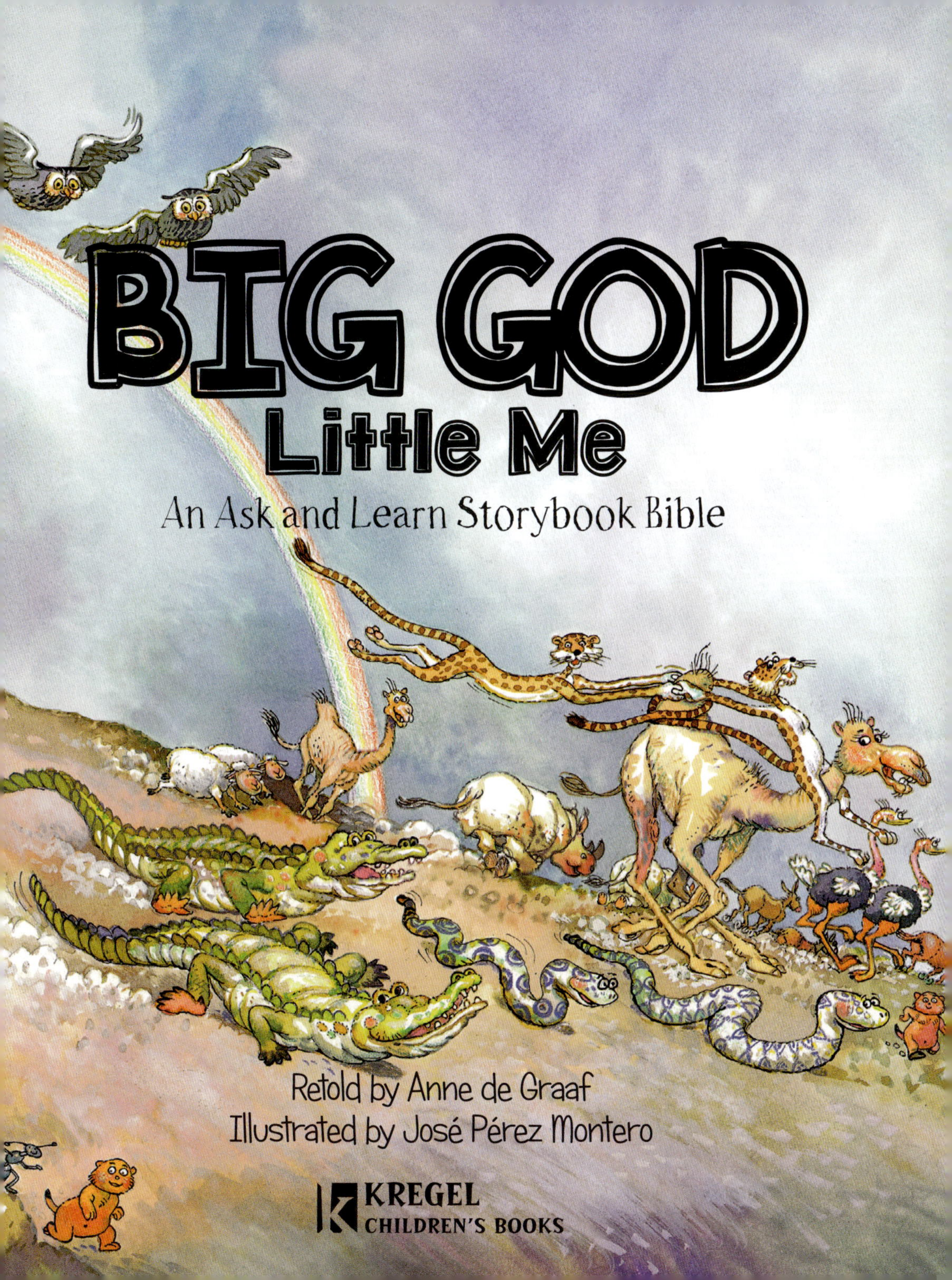

BIG GOD
Little Me

An Ask and Learn Storybook Bible

Retold by Anne de Graaf
Illustrated by José Pérez Montero

KREGEL
CHILDREN'S BOOKS

Big God, Little Me: An Ask and Learn Storybook Bible

Published in 2019 by Kregel Children's Books, an imprint of Kregel Publications,
2450 Oak Industrial Dr. NE, Grand Rapids, MI 49505 USA

Drejervej 15, DK 2400 Copenhagen NV, Denmark
www.sph.as info@sph.as

Edited by Cecilie Fodor
Design by Gao Hanyu

Printed in China / ISBN 978-0-8254-4595-8

Dedicated to YOU!

Contents

OLD TESTAMENT

God Makes the World 9
Noah and the Ark 30
Noah and God's Promise 42
Noah and God's Gift 50
The Beginning of the Tower of Babel 54
The End of the Tower of Babel 66
Abraham Follows God 80
Abraham's Great Big Family 88
Joseph and the Colorful Coat 98
Joseph Forgives His Brothers 106
Moses Hears the Call of God 118
Moses Leads God's People 130
Ruth Must Find a New Home 136
God Rewards Ruth's Loyalty 146
God Chooses David 158
David Fights Goliath 170

Jonah Tries to Run from God 182
Jonah and the Big Fish 196
Esther the Beautiful 210
Queen Esther Saves Her People 219

New Testament

Mary and Joseph 227
The First Christmas 237
Simon Peter, the Rock 250
The Miracles of Jesus 264
The Stories of Jesus 276
Jesus and the Children 290
Jesus in Jerusalem 298
The First Easter 308
Paul's Change of Heart 321
God Promises a New World 338

The Old Testament

God Makes the World

Genesis 1–4

Close your eyes. Hold your breath. *Shh.* What do you feel when everything is dark and quiet?

There was nothing in the beginning . . . except for God.

"God called the light 'day,' and the darkness he called 'night'" (Gen. 1:5).

God took the darkness and changed it, so suddenly . . . there was light.

God made the earth. He made the sun and moon, all the planets, and the stars.

How many stars can you count in the night sky? Ten? A hundred? How many stars do you think God made?

God made the oceans and the seas. He made fish and whales and dolphins and all the animals that swim under water.

Can you find a swordfish?
What about a butterfly fish?

God made the land. He made lions and pandas and elephants and all the animals in the sky and on the land.

God, thank You for making so many amazing animals to fill the earth!

When God was done making the animals, He made the first man and called him Adam.

God made a friend who fit just right with Adam. Her name was Eve. God said all the things He made were very good.

"God created mankind in his own image . . .
male and female he created them" (Gen. 1:27).

Adam and Eve lived in a special garden in a place called Eden. God gave them all the fruit trees to eat from except one.

God said, "Don't eat the fruit from this one tree. If you do, you will die."

An evil serpent told Eve, "The fruit won't kill you. God is lying to you."

Adam and Eve chose not to trust God and ate the fruit. They knew they had done something wrong, and they felt bad about it. They tried to hide from God.

How do you feel when you've done something you shouldn't do? What do you do to try to feel better?

God, forgive us when we do bad things and hurt others. Teach us to trust You more.

God came to Adam and Eve and asked what they had done. Because they hadn't trusted God, they had to leave Eden. They never felt as close to God again.

But God went on loving Adam and Eve. He promised to put an end to sin and rebuild His special relationship with them.

Even after they left the garden, God gave two sons to Adam and Eve.

The Bible says, "Children are a gift from the LORD" (Ps. 127:3 NLT). YOU are a big wiggly gift to your mom and dad, too!

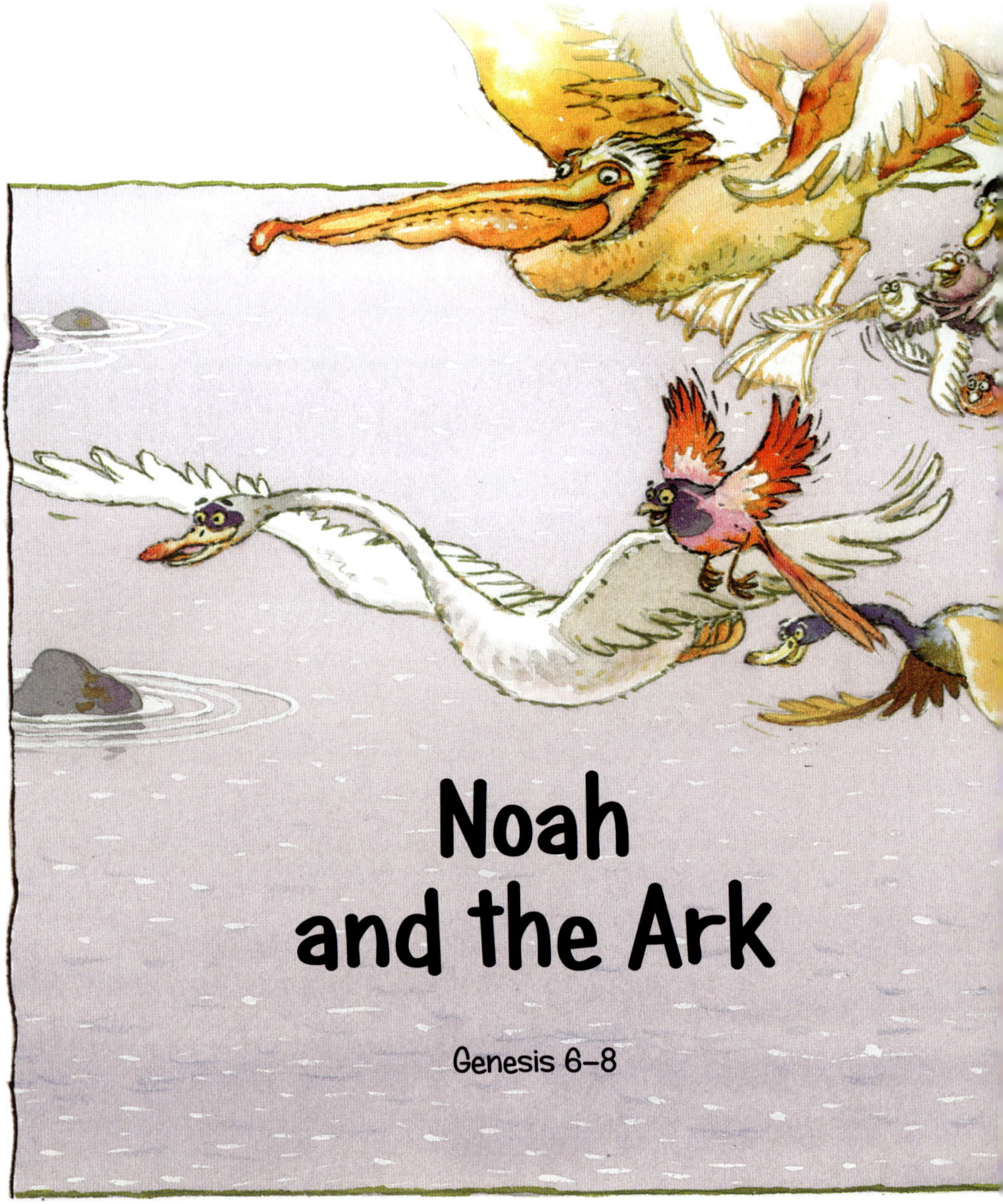

Noah and the Ark

Genesis 6–8

Adam and Eve had
a great-great-great
grandson named Noah.

People had forgotten about God. They were selfish and thought up all kinds of ways to hurt each other.

This made God very sad.

Noah was different. He talked to God and listened to God.

God told Noah, "It's going to rain for a long time, and there will be a huge flood. Build a boat. Build a *really big* boat!"

Noah's boat was called an ark.

The boat had to be so big because God told Noah to take two of every kind of bird and animal on the boat.

God sent the animals to Noah to put on his *really big* boat. God promised to keep Noah, his family, and the animals safe during the huge flood.

How many kinds of animals do you know?

Then, it started to rain and
rain. It rained for forty days
and forty nights.

Count ten fingers. Count ten toes. Do it all over again. That's how many days it rained and rained and rained!

Noah's ark floated higher and higher, higher even than the mountaintops. As water covered the earth, all the living things on the earth drowned.

Finally, the rain stopped.
Then God sent a wind.

Noah and God's Promise

Genesis 8

Water was every-
where! The whole
world looked like
the ocean.

Noah and the animals in the ark waited and waited for the water to go down. Noah sent out a raven, but it couldn't find anywhere to land. So it flew back to the ark.

Then Noah sent out a dove—twice! The second time, the dove returned with an olive leaf in its beak. Somewhere there were places dry enough for plants to grow!

When the earth was dry, God said to Noah, "You, your family, and all the animals may leave the ark. Go on the land and build homes."

So they all came out of the ark.

God kept His promise to them. He kept Noah and his family and all the animals safe and sound.

Noah and God's Gift

Genesis 8–9

Noah thanked God for keeping them safe.
Then God showed Noah a gift.

God's gift to Noah was the rainbow. This was God's sign that He would never flood the whole world again, and that He always keeps His promises.

God, thank You for keeping Your promise to Noah. Thank You that You keep Your promises to us too.

The Beginning of the Tower of Babel

Genesis 11

Where do you live? What country? Do you know how to say "Hi!" in any other languages?

"Mhoro!" "Czesc!" "Hola!" That's how to say "Hi!" in Shona, Polish, and Spanish!

A long, long time ago, everyone spoke the same language. Everyone could say "Hi!" to everyone else.

Then some people moved east, found a flat place, and decided to make it their home.

Where is your home? Do you live somewhere flat or somewhere with hills and mountains?

The people said, "Let's make bricks and bake them until they're very hard."

What happens when you kick a tower made of blocks? *Crash!*

What happens when you kick a tower made of bricks? *Ouch!*

The people were clever. Instead of using stones, they made bricks. They stuck the bricks together with tar instead of mortar.

With bricks and tar, they could make bigger buildings than they could before.

Build a tower with
your fists, one on
top of the other,
on top of the other,
on top of the other. . .
Where will
it stop?

The End of the Tower of Babel

Genesis 11

What is a famous city you know of? How big is it?

The people said, "Let's build a huge city. We will be famous and won't have to wander anymore."

They planned to build a tower so tall that it would reach into the sky. The people thought all their neighbors would be impressed.

People still build huge towers today. Some of them are half a mile high!

When God saw what the people wer
doing, He knew He had to stop them,
or they would think they could do
anything they planned to do.

"The LORD said, 'If as one people speaking the same language they have begun to do this, then nothing they plan to do will be impossible for them" (Gen. 11:6).

So God mixed up their words and made different languages. The people no longer spoke one language but many.

The people couldn't understand each other, so they couldn't finish the city. People called the city Babel, which means "mixed up," because God mixed up the language of the whole world.

God, thank You for languages so we can talk to each other. Teach us to make plans with You, not without You. We don't want to become too proud and think that we can do everything on our own.

God scattered people all over the earth, where they speak all kinds of different languages.

"Goodbye!"
"Adiós!"
"Czesc!"
"Chisaraizvakanaka!"

Abraham Follows God

Genesis 12

Abraham's name means "father of many." His wife's name, Sarah, means "princess." What name did your parents give you? What does your name mean?

Many years later, there was a man named Abraham. He had many sheep, goats, and camels. He and his wife, Sarah, lived near a city called Harran.

How many sheep can you count?
How many goats do Abraham and
Sarah have?

One night, God told Abraham He would make his family into a great nation. His family would bless all peoples scattered across the whole world. Abraham believed God's words and trusted Him.

God told Abraham and Sarah to leave their home and go to a new land that He would give to them. So they packed everything they had onto camels and traveled until God told them when and where to stop.

Abraham and Sarah moved about four hundred miles. Have you ever moved before?

Abraham's Great Big Family

Genesis 15, 18, 21

Many years went by and Abraham and Sarah still didn't have a child and a family of their own. They asked God, "Why?"
God said, "Look up into the sky. How many stars can you count? A million? Ten million? This is how great a family I will give you."

One day, three strangers visited Abraham and Sarah. They welcomed the strangers and served them their best food. But they didn't know one of the visitors was really God.

God told Abraham that Sarah would soon have a son.

Do people come and visit your house? What would you do to make visitors feel welcome?

Sarah was listening from inside the tent. She laughed because she was now very old—too old to have a baby.

The visitor said, "Why did Sarah laugh? Nothing is too hard for God to do."

The visitor told Sarah that He would return in one year. In a year, Sarah would hold her own son in her arms.

A year later, Abraham and Sarah finally had their little boy, Isaac, God's own gift. Isaac was the beginning of the great big family God promised Abraham and Sarah. Isaac's name means "laughter."

God, thank You for giving us good gifts in Your own time. Please teach us to be patient and to wait for the good things You have for us.

Joseph and the Colorful Coat

Genesis 37

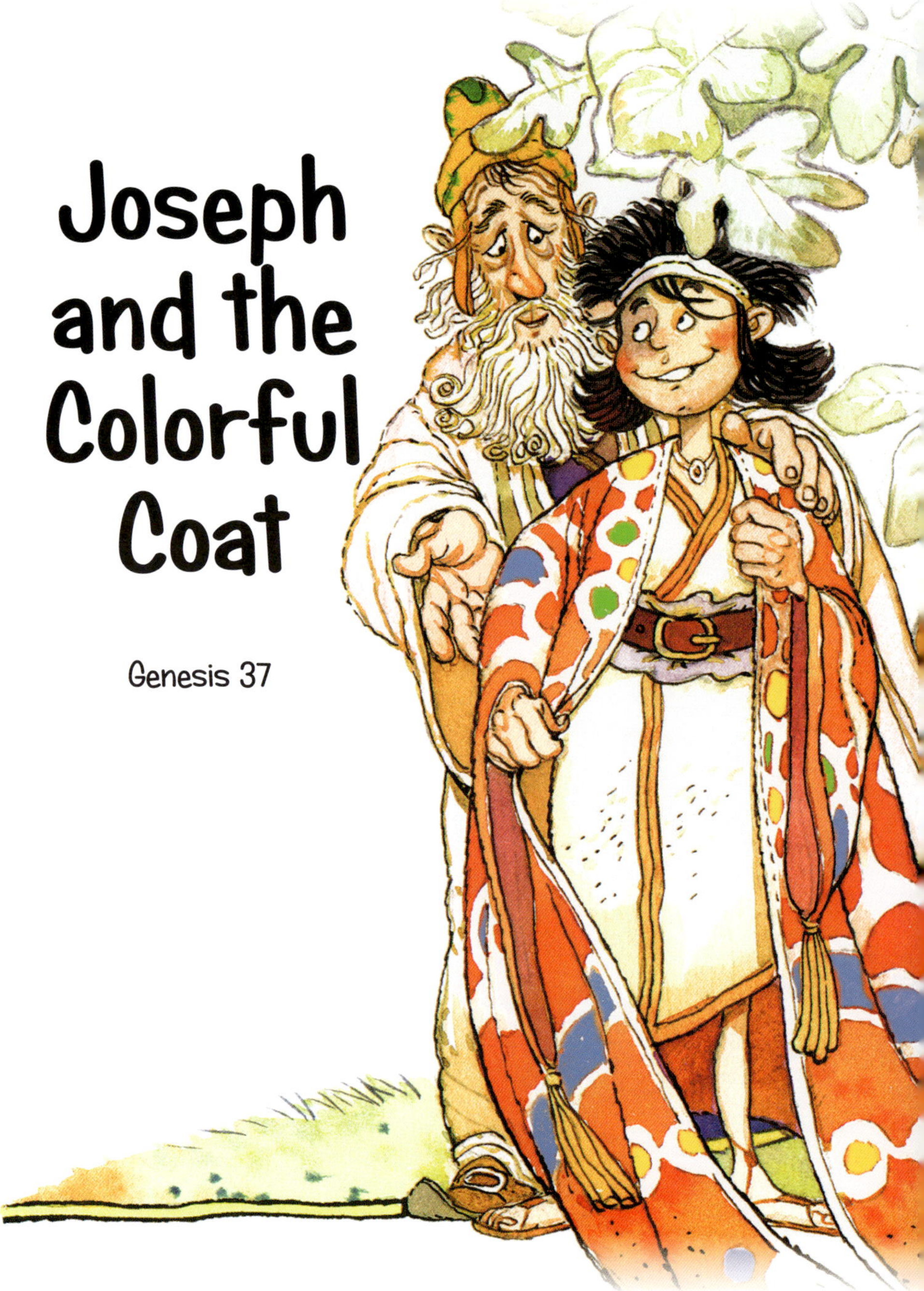

Isaac had a son named Jacob.
Jacob grew up and had twelve sons.
Joseph was his favorite son.
Jacob gave Joseph a special coat.
This made Joseph's brothers jealous.

Have you had a strange dream before?
What did you dream about?

One night, Joseph dreamed the sun, moon, and eleven stars bowed down to him as if he were a king. He thought the dream meant his father, mother, and brothers would one day bow down to him.

His older brothers did not like his dream. "We'll never bow down to you!"

One day, Jacob sent Joseph to check on his brothers. They had taken the sheep into the fields to graze.

"Here comes that dreamer!" his brothers said. They wanted to hurt him, so they took his special coat and threw him in a well.

Has your brother, sister, or friend ever hurt you? Why do you think they wanted to hurt you?

Joseph's brothers sold him as a slave, and he was taken to Egypt—far, far away. But God was with Joseph.

Slaves are not free like you and me. Some people are forced to work without getting money in return.

Joseph Forgives His Brothers

Genesis 39–46

Joseph worked very hard as a slave in Egypt. Because God was with Joseph and helped him, the man who owned Joseph put him in charge of his home and everything he had. Joseph did all his work for God and thought of God as his real master.

In Egypt, God helped Joseph see what dreams meant. Pharaoh, the king of Egypt, told Joseph about a dream where seven fat cows came out of a river and ate the grass on the riverbank.

Then seven skinny cows came and ate up the fat cows, but they stayed skinny!

Count all the fat cows. Count all the skinny cows. How many are there altogether?

God showed Joseph that the seven fat cows stood for seven good years for growing food and raising animals.

So Pharaoh freed Joseph and put him in charge of storing food.

After the seven good years came seven bad years when food wouldn't grow. That's what the skinny cows meant!

Because it was so hard to find food, Joseph's brothers traveled a long, long way to Egypt. They did not recognize Joseph after so many years, but Joseph recognized them.

The last time Joseph's brothers saw him, he was wearing different clothes and speaking a different language!

Do you know anyone who seems different when they wear other clothes, change their hair, or speak different words?

Joseph forgave his brothers for hurting him and selling him as a slave. God had taken care of Joseph—that was what mattered!

Joseph told them, "You wanted to hurt me, but God made the best of it so we could store up lots of food and save many people."

God, thank You for forgiving us when we do bad things and hurt others. Teach us to forgive those who have hurt us, too.

Jacob and his sons moved to Egypt to be near Joseph. Now their whole family was together again!

When do you get to see all of your family?

Moses Hears the Call of God

Exodus 1–4

Many years after Joseph, there was a little baby named Moses. He was much smaller than you when his mother saved his life.

Joseph and his brothers had so many children in Egypt that they became a great nation, just as God promised Abraham.

Pharaoh, the king of Egypt, was afraid of them. He decided to hurt Hebrew babies like Moses. So his mother put him in a basket and sent him floating down a river.

God kept Moses safe. Pharaoh's daughter, the princess, heard Moses crying among the reeds. She saved him and raised him as her son. He grew up in the palace like a prince.

The Egyptians hated the Hebrews and made them into slaves. One day, Moses saw an Egyptian hitting a Hebrew man—one of his people. Moses killed the Egyptian.

When Pharaoh heard this, he tried to kill Moses, but Moses ran away.

Moses hid in the desert in a place called Midian. He was there for forty years!

One day, when Moses was tending sheep in Midian, he saw a bush on fire, but the fire was not burning up the bush! How could that be?

God called out from the bush, "Moses!"

"Here *I* am," Moses said.

God told Moses to go back to Egypt and help save God's people from the Egyptians. But Moses was afraid and said, "Not me, God."

God knew Moses was afraid, so God promised to help him and teach him what to say and what to do.

Moses was still scared, so God said his brother, Aaron, would help him save the Hebrews.

What is something good that you are scared to do? Who could help you do it?

Moses Leads God's People

Exodus 5–20, 34;
Numbers 13–14;
Deuteronomy 1

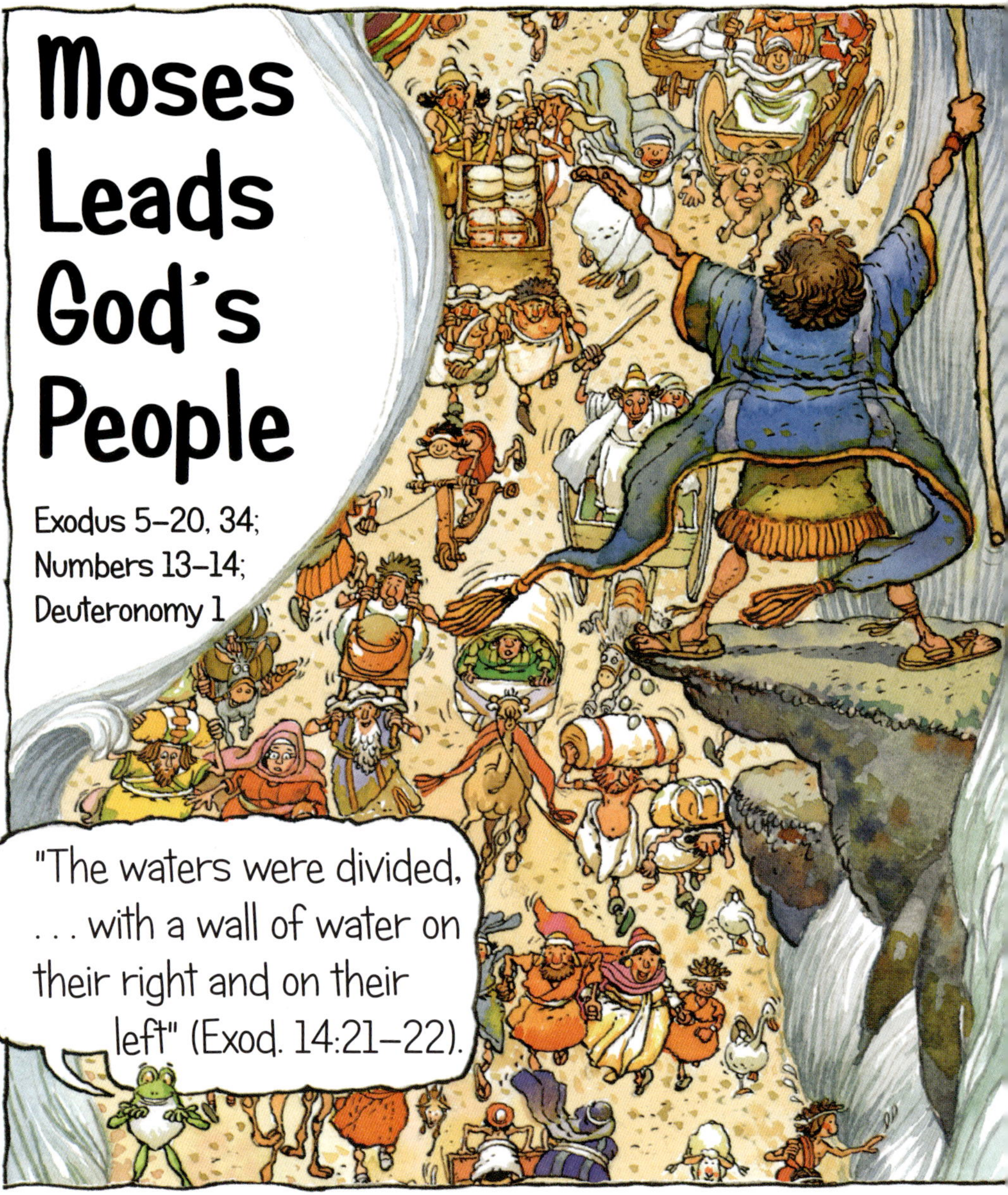

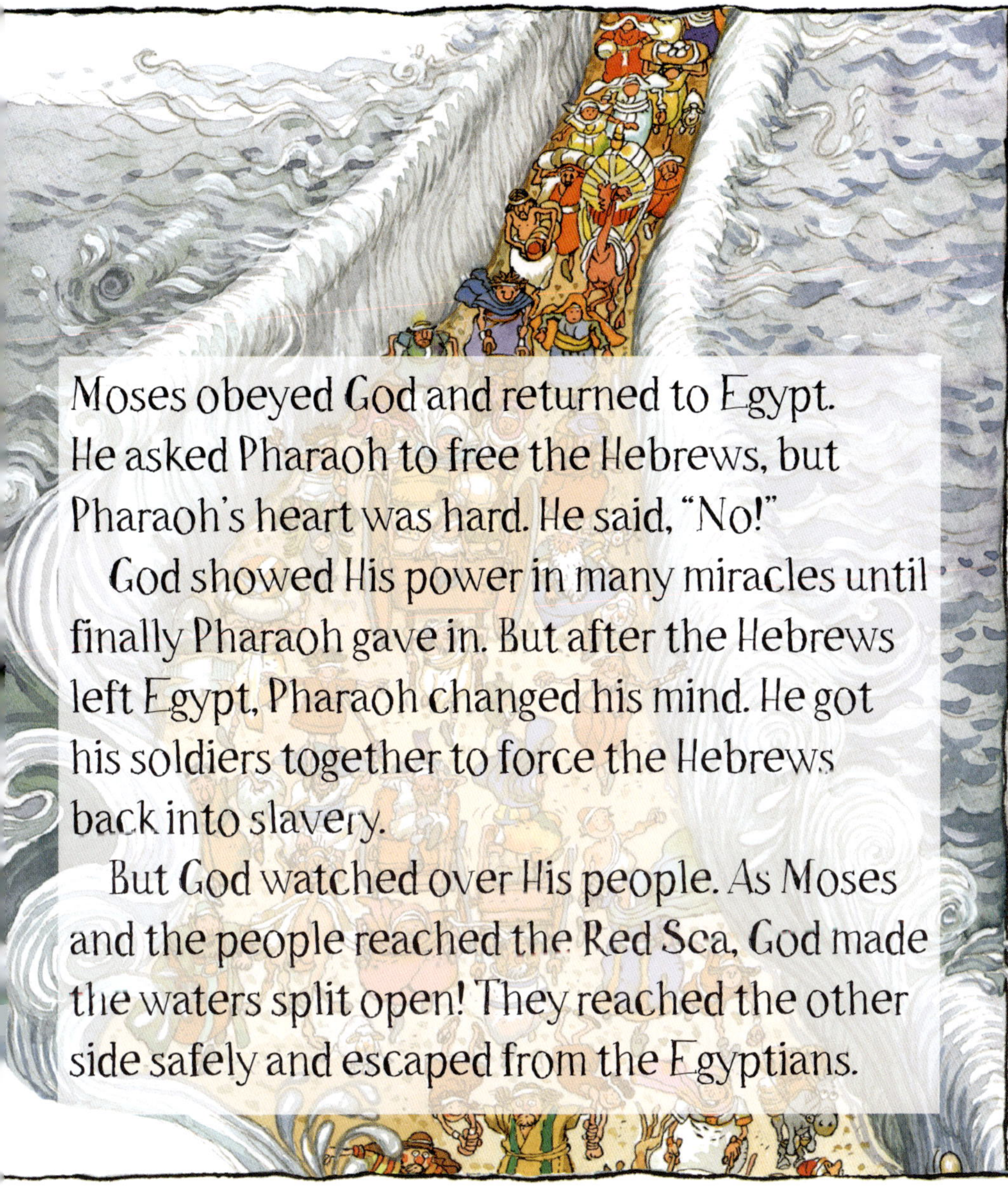

Moses obeyed God and returned to Egypt. He asked Pharaoh to free the Hebrews, but Pharaoh's heart was hard. He said, "No!"

God showed His power in many miracles until finally Pharaoh gave in. But after the Hebrews left Egypt, Pharaoh changed his mind. He got his soldiers together to force the Hebrews back into slavery.

But God watched over His people. As Moses and the people reached the Red Sea, God made the waters split open! They reached the other side safely and escaped from the Egyptians.

It was a long journey to the land God promised to Abraham. The journey was so long the people started to ask whether God would really take care of them.

For God's people to live with Him, God wanted them to trust Him and live differently than they used to live. God wrote ten rules in stone for Moses and His people to follow.

God, please teach us to trust You. You made food and water, all the things we need to build our houses, and the land where we live. Thank You for going with us wherever we are.

When the people arrived in the land God promised them, they still didn't believe God would keep them safe. They grumbled against God.

Instead of entering the Promised Land, God's people had to wander in the desert for forty years. Every day they had to trust God for the food and water they needed.

Ruth Must Find a New Home

Ruth 1

Long after God's people finally entered the Promised Land, there was a woman named Ruth.

One day, Ruth's husband died.

His mother, Naomi, told Ruth, "You should go back home to your own parents." Naomi wanted to return to her home, and God's people, in Israel.

What country were you born in? Is that the same country you live in now?

Although Ruth was very sad, she believed in God and loved God. She also loved Naomi, who had taught her to love God.

Who has taught you to love God?

Ruth begged Naomi, "Please let me go to Israel with you. I will go where you go. Your people will be my people, and your God will be my God. He will take care of us."

Ruth and Naomi had to travel about thirty miles to get to Israel. They also had to cross a big river called the Jordan.

Naomi was very sad because her husband and sons had died. She said, "I went away full, but I have come back empty." She didn't think life would ever get better again.

Naomi and Ruth walked the long, long way to Bethlehem, the city where Naomi was born. Bethlehem would be their new home!

God Rewards Ruth's Loyalty

Ruth 2–4

In Bethlehem, Ruth took care of Naomi. She went into the fields to gather grain and shared it with Naomi.

The field where Ruth gathered grain belonged to a man named Boaz.

Boaz wanted to help Ruth because she was so kind to Naomi.

Boaz let Ruth take home as much grain as she could gather. Naomi said, "Does Boaz own the field? He is a relative of mine!"

Naomi told Ruth, "Because Boaz is from my family and cares about us, maybe he will marry you. He would provide well for you."

God cares for you and your family. What all has God given you?

Ruth and Boaz were married and there was a big party. Naomi was very, very happy!

Can you find someone playing music? How about someone dancing? Is anyone eating? Ruth and Boaz wanted all their friends to celebrate with them!

Now Ruth and Boaz could take care of Naomi together. After a while, they had a little baby boy named Obed. Naomi cared for Obed like he was her own son.

Many, many years later, King David was born in Bethlehem. Obed was David's grandfather.

Many, many years after that, Jesus was born in Bethlehem. They were both part of the same great family that came from Abraham.

God, thank You for giving us families and people who take care of us. Teach us to take care of those who are in need in our families and neighborhoods.
F. Montero

God Chooses David

1 Samuel 16–17

God looked at the heart of a shepherd boy named David, and He saw that David loved Him very much.

David liked to play his harp
and sing songs for God.

What songs do you know
that you can sing for God? Sing one now!

What is one thing that you are very good at?

David was also very good at slinging stones. He could hit whatever he aimed at. He could kill bears that hunted his sheep!

He could even kill lions with his sling!

Count how many sheep David saved from the lion!

A wise man named Samuel came to David's family to find the person God had chosen to be king of Israel.

David's father brought his sons to Samuel, but none of them were God's choice. Not this brother, or this one, or even this one!

How many brothers and sisters do you have?

"Are these seven boys all of your sons?" Samuel asked.

"No," David's father said. "I have one more, my youngest, named David."

Samuel chose David because God had plans for him. Someday David would become king.

"People look at the outward appearance, but the LORD looks at the heart" (1 Sam. 16:7).

David Fights Goliath

1 Samuel 17

Who's the tallest person you know?

The army of Israel was strong, but still the soldiers were very, very scared of the giant Goliath!
The Bible says Goliath was almost ten feet tall!

No one in the army dared to fight Goliath.

David was too small to be a soldier in the army like his brothers, but he begged King Saul, "Let me fight Goliath! God is with me, and *I'm* good with a sling."

"Go, and God be with you," King Saul said.

Goliath was making fun of the Israelites and their God. "You're all scaredy-cats, and so is your God!"

David said, "Oh yeah? You're not too big for my God!"

Has anyone ever made fun of you because you are smaller or younger? How did it make you feel? What did you do?

David took aim at the giant and sent a stone flying through the air with his sling. The stone flew across the field until . . . *THUNK!* It hit Goliath in the head and he fell flat on the ground!

David didn't win because he was bigger or stronger than Goliath. He won because God was with him, and he trusted God.

After David killed Goliath, everyone said, "Three cheers for young David! Hip, hip, hooray! Young David is so brave and handsome."

God, thank You that You are with us even when we are scared or don't feel strong. Help us remember that it's not about how things look on the outside. The most important thing is that You are by our side.

Jonah Tries to Run from God

Jonah 1

Many years after David was king, there was a man named Jonah. God told him to go to the wicked city of Nineveh. "Go warn your enemies to change their ways."

"Warn my enemies?" Jonah said. "I don't want to warn those wicked Ninevites. I want God to punish them."

So Jonah didn't go to Nineveh. He went the other way, toward a city called Tarshish.

Jonah went to Joppa, got on a ship, and sailed for Tarshish. He thought he could run away from God.

But Jonah couldn't run away from God. God is everywhere. Jonah disobeyed, so God sent a great storm that rocked the whole ship.
The Bible says there's nowhere that God can't find us. "Where can I flee from your presence? . . . If I rise on the wings of the dawn, if I settle on the far side of the sea, even there your hand will guide me" (Ps. 139:7, 9–10).

The sailors didn't know what to do! They threw all the heavy cargo overboard, but still the ship was sinking.

They woke up Jonah, who was taking a nap. "What did you do to make God send this terrible storm?" they said.

Jonah told the sailors that God in heaven made both the seas and the land. The sailors didn't know that God is master of everything on the earth!

Jonah said, "This storm is all my fault. Throw me overboard and the seas will become calm again."

The sailors didn't want to hurt Jonah, but they had no choice.

They picked up Jonah and *one, two, three, heave ho!* Into the raging sea he went with a great big splash!

When the seas calmed, the sailors believed in God. They worshiped Him and promised that they would follow Him.

Down, down, down into the sea Jonah went. The storm stopped, but Jonah didn't notice since God provided a huge fish to swallow him up.

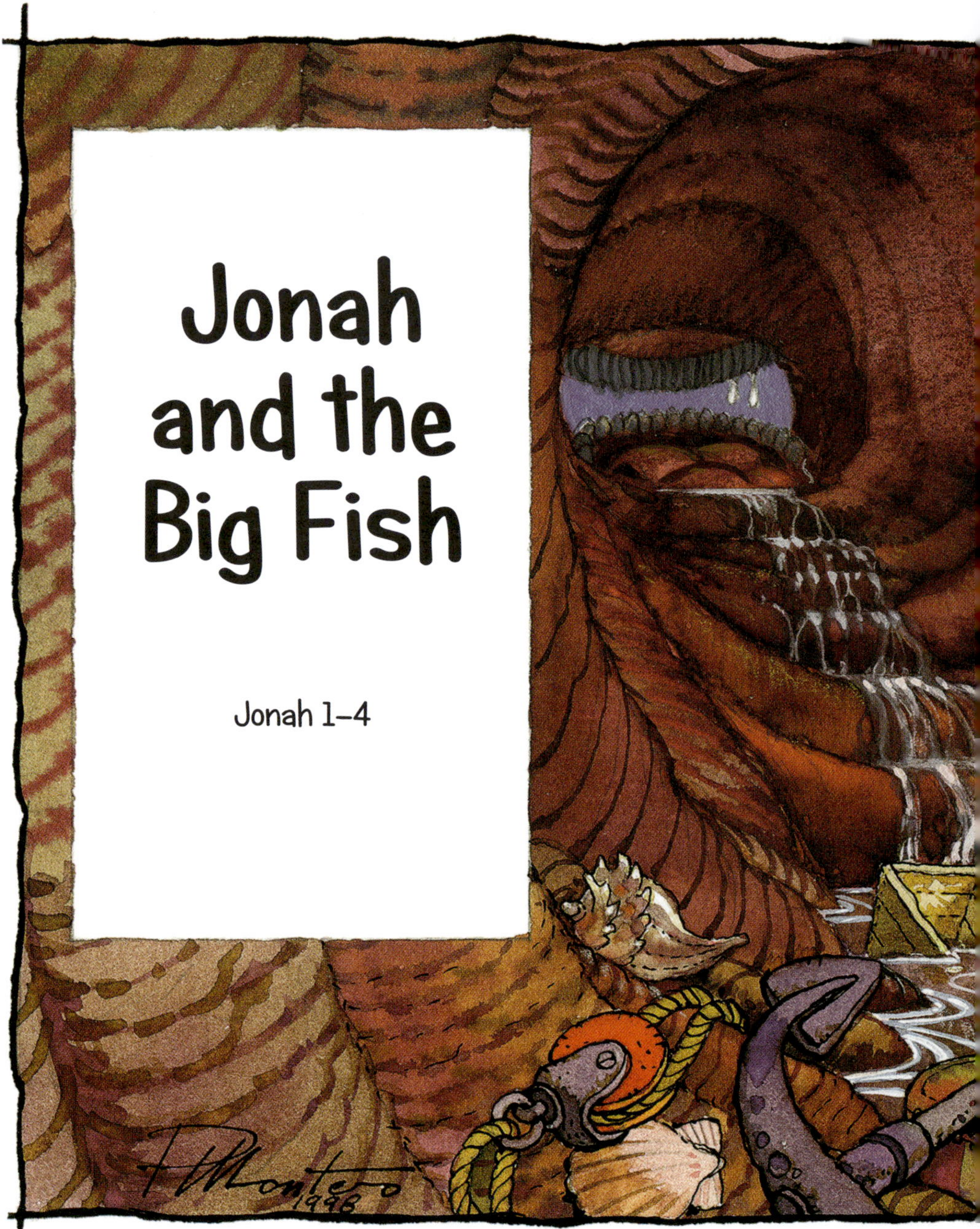

Jonah and the Big Fish

Jonah 1–4

GULP! The huge fish swallowed Jonah. For three days and nights he stayed in the big fish's belly. Jonah prayed and called to God for help. God had the fish spit him out on a beach.

What do you need God's help to do in your life?

God still wanted Jonah to go to Nineveh—not Tarshish or anywhere else. So what did Jonah do this time? Finally, he went to Nineveh!

Guess what? The Ninevites listened! "Oh! We're so sorry!" they cried. They put on clothes that looked like sacks to show God how sorry they were.

How do you show that you are sorry
when you've hurt someone?

The king was sorry too. He took off his rich robes and put on sackcloth like the rest of the Ninevites.

"We should stop hurting others and stop doing wicked things," the king said. "Let everyone pray and ask God to forgive us."

God forgave the Ninevites, but Jonah wasn't happy. He was mad that God had forgiven his enemies instead of punishing them.

Jonah went off by himself outside the city. God made a plant grow up to shade Jonah from the hot sun.

Then God had a worm kill the plant. Now Jonah was *really* mad.

But God told Jonah, "You cared about this plant, and you are mad that it died. But think about how much more *I* care about all those men and women and children in the city! This is why *I* sent you to Nineveh."

God, we're sorry that we don't always listen to You. We're sorry that sometimes we want You to punish people we don't like instead of wanting You to forgive them.

Please teach us to forgive others, and to care about them as people who You love.

Esther the Beautiful

Esther 1–2

There once was a king in the land of Persia who searched far and wide for a queen.

The king had all the most beautiful women in the land brought to his palace. There, they waited a year to hear who the king would choose as his queen. They ate the best food and wore the prettiest makeup and sweetest perfumes.

One of the young women brought to the palace was named Esther. She was different from the others, and not just because she was so beautiful. Esther was keeping a special secret: she was a Jew, one of God's chosen people.

What is your most fun, all-time favorite secret? Come on, you can tell me!

When it was Esther's turn to meet the king, there was no contest! He liked her more than all the other young women in the palace. She became his queen.

Queen Esther Saves Her People

Esther 3–9

One of the king's advisors, a man named Haman, hated the Jews. He said that all the Jewish people in the land should be killed! So the Jews prayed to God, asking for help.

The king loved Esther, but he did not know she was Jewish. When Haman's terrible law ordered all Jews to be killed, Esther prayed to God, then she went to the king.

The king was pleased to see Esther. "What is it, Queen Esther? You can ask me for anything you want." Esther invited the king to dinner, and there she told the king everything!

The king made a new law to save Esther and the Jewish people. The Jews threw a huge party called Purim, in honor of how God used brave Esther to save the Jewish people. Even today, Purim is celebrated by the giving of gifts.

The New Testament

Mary and Joseph

Matthew 1; Luke 1–2

The Christmas story began with a girl named Mary. An angel appeared to her and said, "Mary, you are very special. God is with you and has chosen you to become the mother of Jesus, God's Son."

How would you feel if an angel appeared to you? Most people in the Bible who met angels were afraid of them. But the angels told them not to fear.

God also sent an angel in a dream to a man named Joseph. He was going to be married to Mary.

The angel said, "Don't be afraid to make Mary your wife. She is telling the truth about her baby. He is God's Son. You will call him Jesus."

The name Jesus means "The Lord saves." He was called this because Jesus came to earth to save us from sin and rebuild the special relationship God wants to have with us.

When Jesus was almost ready to be born, Mary and Joseph had to travel all the way from Nazareth to Bethlehem. It took a long time—at least four days!

When Mary and Joseph arrived in Bethlehem, there was no place for them to stay. Many other people were traveling to Bethlehem too, and the city was full of people. Everywhere they tried, they heard the same thing: "No room!"

People traveled with all kinds of animals. Can you find a camel? How about a donkey?

The First Christmas

Matthew 2; Luke 2

On the night Jesus was born, shepherds were in the nearby fields. An angel appeared to them in a bright light.

A Savior is born in Bethlehem!" the angel said.

Then many angels appeared and praised God.

Glory to God! Peace on earth!"

The shepherds hurried to Bethlehem to see what the angels had told them about. "Look!"

They found a place where animals were kept. Inside were Mary and Joseph and the tiny, newborn baby Jesus lying in a feeding trough.

Mary and Joseph took baby Jesus to the temple in Jerusalem. There, an old man of God named Simeon took Jesus in his arms. He said, "Now *I* have seen the Light who will save all people."

An old prophet named Anna came up. She said, "Yes! This is the Savior of our people."

Prophets like Anna and Simeon spoke with God and told others what they had heard from God.

Wise men who lived far away to the east saw a special star in the sky. They knew the King of the Jews had been born. They followed the star and rode a long way to Bethlehem to find the young Jesus.

Many stars have names and make special shapes called "constellations." Do you know the names of any constellations?

The wise men bowed down to Jesus and brought Him wonderful gifts fit for a king.

They gave Jesus gold, a rich perfume called myrrh, and frankincense, which smells sweet when burned.

Jesus is called the Light of the world. On that first Christmas, Jesus was God's present to all of us.

Simon Peter, the Rock

Matthew 4–10, 16; Acts 15

Do you know what a fisherman catches?

Jesus grew up and became a special teacher called a "rabbi."

At that time, there was a fisherman named Simon. One day, Simon was fishing with his brother. Jesus called them: "Come, follow Me, and I will send you out to fish for people." Jesus chose Simon plus eleven others to be His closest followers, or "disciples."

Can you count how many disciples there were?

Simon followed Jesus from village to village. He listened to Jesus teach about the kingdom of heaven. Jesus had good news to share about how much God loves us, and what the world would look like if we all loved others as God loves us.

Jesus taught, "Love is the greatest commandment."

The crowds grew larger and larger as Jesus taught. "Follow Me," He called to all the people.

Many men, women, and children followed Jesus, learning from Him and supporting His ministry.

Simon watched Jesus help blind people see and lame people walk. Simon could not believe his eyes. It was a miracle!

Many years before Jesus was born, the prophet Isaiah said that Jesus would bring good news for the poor, give sight to the blind, free those in prison, and save people who were treated unfairly (Luke 4:18). The people of Israel were excited Jesus had finally come!

Simon followed Jesus for over two years. The more he listened to Jesus, the more he loved Him. One day Jesus told him, "Your name is Simon, but from now on you will be called Peter." Peter means "rock."

Jesus said, "Someday you will lead the people who follow Me. They are My church. You will become the rock on which the church is built."

Peter followed Jesus and spent the rest of his life helping others follow Jesus. Later in life, he bravely led the Christians. Peter became a true fisher of people.

Do you know what a "fisher of people" catches?

The Miracles of Jesus

Matthew 8–9; Mark 2; Luke 5, 17; John 2, 11

A miracle is something God makes happen even when people think it's impossible.

At a wedding, Mary asked her son Jesus to help when the wine was all gone. So Jesus turned water into wine!

Once Jesus was inside a house, teaching. There were so many people that no one could get through the door.

Some men had a friend who couldn't walk. They cut a hole in the roof and lowered their friend into the house!

"Get up and walk!" Jesus said, and the man was healed.

What's something you want to do that you need your friends to help you with?

Why do you think Jesus wasn't afraid of the storm?

One day, Jesus and His disciples were out sailing when a storm suddenly came up. Huge waves crashed over the boat. The disciples were afraid they would all drown. But Jesus was fast asleep on a pillow.

Just as God calmed the storm for Jonah, Jesus calmed the storm for His friends. "God and I are one and the same," Jesus told them.

The disciples woke up Jesus. He told the wind and the waves to be quiet—and they were!

Later, Jesus met ten very sick men. They were so sick that no one wanted to touch them.

"Please help us!" they begged Jesus.

So Jesus healed them. Only one man came back to say thank you to Jesus.

One day, a woman who was sick reached through the crowd and touched Jesus's robe. Immediately she was healed! Jesus felt her touch and said, "Your faith has made you whole."

Mary, Martha, and their brother, Lazarus, were all good friends of Jesus.

Once while Jesus was traveling, Lazarus became very sick and died. Mary and Martha were so sad. But Jesus came to their house and made Lazarus live again!

God, thank You that You are so strong that You can do things that sound impossible to us.

Teach us to trust You for the things we need and want. We know You don't fix everything that hurts us now, so help us to wait for Your perfect timing.

The Stories of Jesus

Matthew 7; Luke 11–12, 15; John 10

Jesus taught about God's love by telling stories. These are just a few of the stories He told.

Jesus said not to worry about our food and clothes. He told His followers they were worth far more than the birds that fly and the flowers that grow. God provides food for the birds, and He clothes the flowers in bright colors, so He'll take care of us too.

Do you have a favorite kind of bird or flower?

Jesus told another story about a man who knocked on his neighbor's door late at night. He needed to borrow some bread. He kept knocking and knocking until the man finally opened the door and gave him three loaves.

What happens when you knock on a door? Try it now. When you pray, it is like knocking on God's door. You can always ask God for the things you need. God hears your prayers, no matter how softly you whisper them. You can talk to Him anytime you want to.

Another time, Jesus said everyone who listens to Him and does what He says is like a person who builds a house on solid rock instead of sand.

A house built on sand would wash away in the rain and wind!

Have you ever build a sandcastle on the beach? What happened to it after you left?

Jesus taught that a good shepherd does all he can to save his sheep. He does not run away when a wolf comes.

Jesus meant that He watches over
us and is with us even when bad
things come our way and frighten us.

Jesus told a story of a proud young man who wanted more. He wanted more money, more things, and more friends. He also wanted to travel more, so he left home. This made his father very sad.

What do you want more of?

Soon the young man ran out of money, and all his friends left. So he took a job feeding pigs. The pigs were getting more food than he was, so he went back home.

He thought his father wouldn't be happy to see him because he had wasted all that he had. But his father was overjoyed and welcomed him with open arms.

Jesus and the Children

Matthew 14, 19; John 6

Some people brought little children to Jesus so He could bless them.

Jesus's friends told the children, "Go away. Jesus has more important things to do than spend time with you."

But Jesus said, "No! Let the children come to me."

Jesus liked to teach children of all ages.

Once at the end of a long day of teaching, Jesus's friends said, "Send everyone home. They're all so hungry." But Jesus said He wanted to stay and feed them all.

"But there are thousands of people here!" Jesus's friends said. "We don't have enough food."

A little boy stepped forward. "*I* have five loaves of bread and two fish. *It's* not much, but *I'll* share."

Jesus told all the people to sit down. He looked up to heaven and thanked God for the food. Then Jesus broke the bread into many pieces and gave it to the people.

What a surprise! There was so much bread and so many fish that more than five thousand people ate all they wanted. There were even twelve baskets full of leftovers! Jesus had provided more than they could imagine.

Jesus in Jerusalem

Matthew 26–27;
Luke 19, 22–23;
John 18

When Jesus entered Jerusalem, all the people cheered for Him. They waved palm branches up and down. They threw their coats on the ground before Him. They shouted, "Hosanna!" They thought Jesus had come to be their king and fight their enemies.

But the temple leaders did not like Jesus. They thought Jesus was going to take away their power and their money.

They paid one of Jesus's friends, Judas, thirty pieces of silver to help them trap Jesus.

Have you ever been mean to your friend before? What happened?

This is why people break bread and drink wine together at church, to remember Jesus.

That night, Jesus and His friends shared a special meal called Passover. They remembered how God rescued Moses and the Hebrew people from slavery in Egypt.

Jesus gave bread and wine to His friends. "This is a new promise," He said. "Just as God rescued the Hebrews, *I* will rescue you from your sin."

After the Last Supper, Jesus went out to a garden with His friends to pray.

Judas led Jesus's enemies right to Him. Peter fought back! He cut off the ear of one of the men. But Jesus taught people to love their enemies. He touched the man's ear and healed him.

Can you find Jesus's friends? Where do you think they are going?

Jesus's enemies brought Him to a judge. They lied and said Jesus had done all kinds of bad things. "Kill Him on a cross!" they screamed.

The First Easter

Matthew 27–28; Luke 24; John 21; Acts 1

Jesus's enemies nailed Him to a cross, where He died. His friends and family cried and were very sad. They took His body down from the cross and placed Him in a special cave with a huge stone for a door. Guards stood outside the cave to keep the body safe.

Jesus once taught that a seed has to go underneath the ground, where it is very dark, before a tree can grow up and bear new seeds.

When Jesus died, everything seemed very dark—just like it will be inside my cocoon.

A few days later, some women who were Jesus's friends came back to the cave. It was empty!

"Where is Jesus?" they cried. The guards didn't know where He was.

A huge stone stood in front of the cave so no one would go inside. The women knew they wouldn't be able to move the stone on their own. But an angel rolled away the stone and sat on top of it!

An angel appeared to them. "Fear not!" the angel said. "Are you looking for Jesus? He is alive again! He is not dead. Be happy! Go into the cave and see where He used to lie. Now go tell everyone that He's alive."

The women ran off, hardly believing their eyes and ears.

Look at what happened to me! Isn't it a miracle that a catcrpillar can go inlo a cocoon and come out a butterfly?

After Jesus rose from the dead, He visited His friends. They were out fishing. They had fished all night and caught nothing.

Then Jesus said to them, "Throw your net out again!" This time they caught so many fish the net almost burst!

When Jesus's friends realized He had come back from the dead, Peter jumped out of the boat and swam to shore to see Jesus. They were so excited to see Him again!
Have you ever been excited to see someone again? What did you do when you saw them?

Jesus spent forty days visiting and teaching His friends.

"Go tell everyone the good news about Me, that *I* have come to save you from your sin!" Jesus said. "Teach everyone to love God and love their neighbors as themselves. And My Spirit will be with you always."

Then Jesus left them and went up to heaven.

Jesus, thank You for dying for us—and for coming back to life! You are our light and our hope. Thank You for sending Your Spirit to be with us even today.
Help us to share the good news that You came to save us from our sin, because You love us and want to be with us.

Paul's Change of Heart

Acts 7–9, 11, 13–28

Paul thought Jesus and His friends were liars. So he hurt Jesus's friends and tried to make them stop talking about Jesus.

Has someone tried to hurt your friends before?

Paul left Jerusalem and went to another city to hurt more of Jesus's friends. But on his way, a bright light blinded him and he fell to the ground!

Paul heard Jesus's voice say to him, "Why are you hurting Me? When you hurt My followers, you hurt Me. I have something better for you to do with your life." Then God helped Paul see that Jesus is the Son of God.

Jesus changed Paul's heart and gave him his sight again. Then Paul traveled far and wide, telling everyone he met about Jesus's love.

Greece and Turkey are two of the countries Paul visited. What places in the world would you like to visit?

Some people didn't like Paul talking about Jesus's love. They cared more about power and making money than loving others.

Jesus's enemies threw Paul and his friend Silas into prison. But even inside prison, Paul and Silas could still pray and sing songs about God's love.

The more Paul talked to people about Jesus, the more Jesus's enemies tried to hurt Paul.

During his many years in jail, Paul wrote letters to his friends. He taught them about Jesus and about God's love.

One day Jesus's enemies arrested Paul. So he had to go to Rome in Italy. To get there, he had to travel by boat.

Then a storm came. The storm raged day after day, night after night. Some of the men wanted to get in the lifeboats and leave the ship, but Paul said, "Unless these men stay on the ship, they cannot be saved!"

The storm lasted for two whole weeks! Most of the sailors didn't eat that entire time. They must have been really tired and hungry afterward.

Paul was shipwrecked on an island called Malta. But soon after, he made it safely to Rome.

Paul started his journey as an enemy of Jesus. But Paul had a change of heart. He ended up traveling far and wide, spreading the good news that Jesus lives and forgives!

God, thank You for people like Paul who take the good news of Jesus to faraway lands. Help us to take the good news about Jesus wherever we go.

God Promises a New World

Revelation 1, 3, 21–22

John was a close friend of Jesus.

When John was an old man, he had a vision, which was a special message from God. John wrote down Jesus's words. Jesus said to him, "I'm here for anyone who asks Me into their lives. I'm standing at the door, knocking, waiting for them to hear My voice and open the door."

Have you ever knocked on someone's door? Did they let you in? Were they excited to see you?

Like the story Jesus told about knocking on God's door when we pray, God is knocking on our door. God wants us to let Him inside, because He loves us and wants to be with us.

In John's vision, he heard music and saw a huge crowd. They were all the followers of Jesus from all times and all countries. No one could count all the people!

How high can you count? There will be even more people with Jesus in the new heaven and new earth!

John's vision shows us what God's kingdom will be like. No one there will do anything bad, and there will be no more sadness.

In John's vision, he saw that those who chose to follow Jesus were there with God. They lived in a new city full of light and happiness.

John often compared God to light. He once wrote to his friends, "God is light; in him there is no darkness at all. . . . If we walk in the light, as he is in the light, we have fellowship with one another" (1 John 1:5, 7).

Jesus said to John, "Listen! *I* am coming soon. *I* was in the beginning of all things, and *I* will be there at the end."

In the beginning there was darkness. In the end with Jesus there is light. Now let's pray together the last words John wrote:

"Amen. Come, Lord Jesus!"

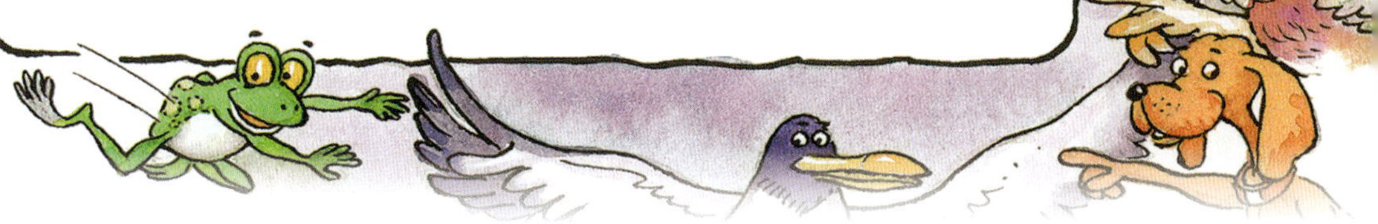